THE LESS-ENERGY REVOLUTION: THE SMARTER POWER ERA OF AI.

Innovations making AI, IoT, and computing faster and the future greener.

Linden L. Sommerfeld

Table of Content

Introduction

We're at a turning point in tech. For years, the push has been for speed, intelligence, and massive data handling. But there's a hidden cost to this progress: power consumption. Every task, from running algorithms in massive data centers to processing data on tiny sensors, eats up energy. And as our tech gets smarter, the energy demands are starting to outweigh what our planet can sustainably provide.

This is where the low-power revolution comes in. It's not just about saving battery life—it's about rethinking the foundation of computing. We're moving toward systems designed to be smarter with energy use, not just faster.

This book explores how energy-efficient hardware, like RISC-V processors, and advanced computing techniques like near-memory computing and parallelism, are reshaping AI, IoT, and more. These aren't just lab experiments—they're powering real-world innovations from medical tools to self-driving vehicles.

Gone are the days when building bigger, faster machines was the answer. The future lies in doing more with less. Imagine AI that matches today's supercomputers in capability but runs on your smartwatch. That future is closer than you think.

This isn't just a book. It's an invitation to witness a silent but powerful shift already reshaping our world. Let's begin.

Chapter 1: The Growing Need for Energy-Efficient Computing

Artificial intelligence and computing technologies have expanded into nearly every area of modern life—from self-driving cars to financial markets that operate at breakneck speeds. AI now plays a vital role in sectors like healthcare, entertainment, and transportation. However, this progress comes at a steep price: the immense energy required to power these technologies.

The rise of edge computing is one way to tackle this challenge—by embedding AI directly into devices like smartphones, wearables, and IoT sensors. These edge devices process data locally, cutting down on latency and the need for continuous data transfers to distant servers. However, these devices can't rely on vast power supplies like large data centers do. Instead, they need to be optimized for efficiency.

For decades, the computing world has been driven by one simple idea: maximize performance. This meant creating bigger servers, faster processors, and more powerful data centers, all of which consumed enormous amounts of electricity. But this approach is no longer viable in a world where sustainability has become paramount.

Today, data centers alone account for over 1% of the global electricity consumption. To put it into perspective, training a large AI model can consume as much energy as an entire city's worth of households over the course of a year. The growing demand for computational power is straining resources, and it's clear we need a shift in direction.

Energy-efficient computing is no longer a luxury—it's a necessity. As AI continues to scale, with billions of devices becoming connected through the Internet of Things (IoT), the power demands of traditional systems will simply become unsustainable. Instead, we need new designs for chips, hardware, and software that prioritize energy efficiency.

The future of AI will depend on those who can deliver exceptional performance while minimizing energy consumption. It's not enough to just make machines faster and smarter; the systems of tomorrow must be built to be sustainable, reducing their environmental footprint while still performing at a high level.

The real challenge of the next decade in computing will be creating platforms that enable AI to function effectively without overwhelming our energy resources. This book delves into how these low-power systems are already starting to take shape, with new chip designs, smarter algorithms, and optimized systems that promise to deliver high performance with minimal energy use.

The rest of the chapter discusses how this shift is already underway, examining new innovations in hardware and software, such as the development of more energy-efficient processors and algorithms that are optimized for low power use.

Chapter 2: Cloud to Edge—The Shift in Computing

Moving AI Closer to the Data Source

Artificial intelligence has long depended on powerful cloud data centers to process large-scale models and handle complex tasks. These data centers are vast, capable of running resource-intensive AI algorithms, offering incredible computational power. However, as AI applications become more pervasive, the trend is shifting. AI no longer needs to rely solely on centralized systems. Instead, it's moving closer to where the data is generated—edge computing.

Edge computing refers to running AI on devices that are at the "edge" of networks—closer to the data source. These devices include everything from smartphones and smartwatches to drones and autonomous vehicles. The main advantage of this shift is the ability to process data in real-time. For applications like autonomous driving, which require instant decisions, waiting for data to travel to the cloud and back isn't an option. In such cases, processing must happen instantly on the device itself.

Real-time decision-making is crucial across various sectors like healthcare, industrial automation, and smart cities. Imagine a smart camera in a city monitoring traffic and adjusting lights for optimal flow. The camera must process data about traffic conditions immediately, not send it back to a server for analysis. This is where edge AI comes in, enabling these devices to process complex data efficiently and make decisions faster.

Overcoming the Challenges of Edge Computing

However, moving AI from the cloud to the edge isn't as simple as just placing powerful chips into tiny devices. These devices often face power limitations that large data centers don't. While a cloud-based data center might have unlimited access to energy and cooling, edge devices need to work with far less power. Most edge devices, such as wearables, operate on batteries, meaning their design needs to focus heavily on energy efficiency.

For AI systems at the edge, the power-to-performance ratio becomes a critical factor. These devices still need to perform complex tasks—like recognizing objects in images or analyzing speech—without draining their batteries. This calls for a new approach to computing, where the emphasis is on smart, power-efficient design. The challenge is to create systems that do more with less energy.

The move to edge computing represents a major transformation in the design and deployment of AI. Traditionally, the industry has focused on scaling up power and performance. But with edge AI, the focus has shifted to scaling intelligently. Rather than pushing devices to operate like cloud servers, edge devices need to perform tasks with minimal energy consumption while maintaining fast, real-time responsiveness.

This shift also opens up new opportunities for AI applications across industries. Consider drones, which previously relied on sending data back to the cloud for processing. Now, many drones can process images, track objects, and even navigate without relying on a central server. This significantly reduces the need for constant cloud communication and lowers energy consumption.

As more devices take on AI tasks at the edge, they will need to become even more efficient in their use of energy. Devices like smartphones, smartwatches, and sensors, which once relied on occasional data updates to the cloud, will need to perform more local processing to keep up with the growing complexity of AI applications.

Despite its advantages, edge computing isn't without challenges. One of the biggest hurdles is the sheer variety of devices and systems that must be optimized for energy efficiency. From low-power sensors to high-performance drones, each device has unique demands for processing power and energy consumption. Developing hardware and software that can scale to meet these diverse needs while keeping power usage in check will require innovation across the entire tech ecosystem.

Moreover, as AI moves to the edge, it brings with it the need for new software architectures and algorithms optimized for these smaller, energy-efficient devices. These algorithms will need to be adapted for edge devices with far fewer resources than those found in a cloud data center.

At the same time, data security and privacy also become even more important. With edge computing, data can be processed locally on devices rather than being sent to the cloud, which can enhance privacy and reduce the risk of data breaches. This decentralized approach has the potential to make AI applications more secure, especially in sensitive fields like healthcare or financial services.

In summary, the shift from cloud-based computing to edge computing is not just about moving workloads closer to the user; it's about a fundamental change in how AI is designed, deployed, and optimized. Edge AI allows for faster decision-making, more efficient energy usage, and more secure applications.

However, it also requires overcoming significant technical challenges, particularly in developing hardware and software that can work efficiently in low-power environments. The future of AI will be defined by systems that are both powerful and energy-conscious, balancing performance with sustainability in ways that were previously unimaginable.

Chapter 3: The Core Principles of Energy-Efficient Computing

Foundations of Low-Power Technology

As computing systems scale in complexity, from advanced AI to Internet of Things (IoT) devices, the need for energy efficiency is becoming crucial. While computational performance has long been the top priority, energy efficiency is now a fundamental necessity. Power-hungry processors and data centers are no longer viable as we look to the future. Energy-efficient systems aren't just about saving power; they ensure the sustainability of technology across industries.

At the core of energy-efficient computing is understanding how power is consumed by systems. One of the key methods for reducing power usage is voltage scaling. Power consumption is proportional to the square of the voltage; even a slight reduction in voltage can lead to significant energy savings. Many modern processors use dynamic voltage and frequency scaling (DVFS), a technique that adjusts the power usage depending on the workload. During idle times, the system operates at lower voltage levels, conserving energy without sacrificing performance.

Another critical principle in low-power design is power gating. Traditional processors continue to draw power even when parts of the system aren't in use, such as idle cores in multi-core processors. Power gating eliminates this waste by shutting off power to unused components, ensuring energy is only consumed by the active parts of the system. This is particularly important for high-performance computing systems, which contain many cores.

Furthermore, memory access in computing systems is one of the largest contributors to energy consumption. Efficient memory management is essential for reducing overall power use. Innovations in memory technologies like near-memory computing allow for computations to occur closer to memory rather than constantly transferring data between the processor and memory. By minimizing these power-hungry memory operations, systems can achieve faster processing while using less energy.

How AI, IoT, and High-Performance Computing Differ

Energy-efficient computing differs significantly across various domains, depending on the specific needs of the system. The power requirements of AI models running on high-performance cloud servers are vastly different from those of small, battery-powered IoT devices. Each domain has its unique set of challenges and demands, yet they all rely on energy-efficient technologies to meet performance goals while conserving power.

In high-performance computing (HPC) environments like data centers, the challenge is scaling up performance without increasing energy consumption excessively. AI workloads in data centers typically require significant processing power, with systems handling vast amounts of data. To optimize for energy use, techniques such as liquid cooling, power-aware workload scheduling, and hardware accelerators like GPUs or specialized AI processors are employed to maximize computational output while minimizing the environmental impact.

In contrast, IoT systems operate in environments where power is extremely limited. These devices must perform AI tasks while consuming very little power. Smart sensors in agriculture, wearable health monitors, and AI-powered appliances rely on ultra-low-power processors to perform functions without constantly draining their batteries. In such systems, efficiency is achieved through techniques like duty cycling (turning off components when not in use) and event-driven processing (activating the device only when necessary).

The edge computing landscape, a blend between the cloud and IoT, has unique power constraints. While edge devices have more processing capability than traditional IoT sensors, they still need to optimize for power efficiency. Devices like autonomous vehicles, smart cameras, and industrial robots must be capable of processing data in real-time while operating on limited power sources. Optimizing these devices requires balancing computational power with energy-efficient hardware and software, ensuring the system remains responsive without draining resources.

Each category of computing—whether it's HPC, IoT, or edge computing—presents its own set of trade-offs in the pursuit of energy efficiency. The ability to tailor hardware and software for the specific needs of each system is key to achieving maximum efficiency.

Achieving the Balance Between Performance and Power

One of the most significant challenges in modern computing is achieving the optimal balance between performance and power. Historically, increasing performance often meant using more power. However, innovations in energy-efficient technologies have begun to prove that these two goals do not need to be mutually exclusive.

Workload management is a critical strategy for balancing performance with power consumption. Not every task requires the same amount of processing power, and adjusting system resources based on the task's intensity helps to optimize energy usage. For example, in AI inference, models can be designed to adjust their complexity based on available power. This means that when power is abundant, the system can ramp up performance, and when power is limited, it scales back, preserving battery life.

In addition to workload management, the rise of task-specific accelerators—processors designed for specific types of computations—has proven essential in maintaining high performance with low power. General-purpose processors tend to waste energy when performing specialized tasks, as they are designed to handle a wide range of workloads. By using domain-specific architectures (DSAs) like AI accelerators, neuromorphic chips, and FPGA-based computing, systems can perform their tasks more efficiently while consuming far less energy.

The design of neural networks can also be optimized for efficiency. Techniques such as neural network pruning, quantization, and sparsity allow AI models to perform complex tasks while reducing the computational load. By eliminating redundant calculations, reducing precision, and focusing on the most important connections in a neural network, these optimizations allow AI to function on low-power hardware.

The future of computing will not just be about building faster processors—it will be about building smarter, more efficient processors. The integration of specialized processors, parallel computing, and adaptive algorithms will shape the next generation of energy-efficient systems that achieve high performance without the energy penalty.

Chapter 4: Innovations in Hardware – RISC-V and Beyond

The Rise of RISC-V and Custom Hardware

In the quest for energy-efficient computing, hardware designers have been pushed to rethink conventional processor architectures. One of the most revolutionary innovations in this area is RISC-V, an open-source instruction set architecture (ISA) that is gaining traction across the tech industry. Unlike proprietary architectures like x86 or ARM, RISC-V offers unprecedented flexibility, scalability, and customizability, making it a game-changer for energy-efficient AI and IoT applications.

RISC-V is based on the Reduced Instruction Set Computing (RISC) philosophy, which simplifies processor instructions to make execution more efficient and consume less power. This modular approach allows developers to tailor processors to specific workloads, ensuring that power-hungry instructions are minimized. This openness and adaptability have led to widespread adoption, with researchers, startups, and major tech giants leveraging RISC-V to create custom processors designed for low-power computing.

The shift toward custom hardware solutions is being driven by the growing demand for processors that can handle specific tasks more efficiently. From ultra-low-power embedded systems to high-performance AI accelerators, the focus is now on domain-specific architectures (DSAs). By designing processors tailored to a particular workload—such as neural network operations or real-time image processing—developers can achieve higher performance while consuming significantly less power.

Architectural Advancements in Low-Power Computing

RISC-V's flexibility is also leading to breakthroughs in hardware architecture. One of the key advantages of RISC-V is its ability to support parallel processing, which allows multiple processing units to work simultaneously. This approach increases computational efficiency and reduces bottlenecks that would typically require high power consumption. Multi-core systems built on RISC-V are particularly well-suited for tasks that can be distributed across multiple processors, making them ideal for AI applications that require massive amounts of parallel computation.

Another architectural innovation driven by RISC-V is the use of shallow pipelines. Traditional processors rely on deep instruction pipelines to achieve high clock speeds, but this often leads to increased power consumption. RISC-V-based processors, on the other hand, utilize simplified pipelines, reducing the overall energy expenditure while maintaining competitive performance. This efficiency is particularly important in low-power environments like mobile devices, where energy consumption must be minimized.

Furthermore, specialized memory hierarchies have become a key component of energy-efficient computing systems. In traditional systems, processors frequently access data stored in memory, which consumes a large amount of power. RISC-V systems are incorporating near-memory computing techniques, which allow for data to be processed directly in memory, reducing the need for expensive data transfers between memory and processing units. This reduces both the latency and power consumption associated with memory-intensive tasks.

The combination of RISC-V's open-source nature, parallel processing, shallow pipelines, and near-memory computing is making it a central player in the next generation of low-power computing systems. These innovations are already making a significant impact on real-world applications, from IoT devices to large-scale AI infrastructures.

From Prototype to Production

RISC-V's journey from research to widespread adoption is a testament to its potential in transforming the hardware industry. What began as an academic initiative has quickly evolved into a commercially viable platform, with companies and institutions around the world developing RISC-V-based processors for a wide range of applications.

One notable example of RISC-V's success is the PULP (Parallel Ultra-Low Power) platform. This open-source computing initiative demonstrates the ability of RISC-V to deliver high-performance computing with minimal energy consumption. PULP has been successfully implemented in AI-driven medical devices, industrial automation, and environmental monitoring systems, proving that low-power AI accelerators based on RISC-V can power real-world solutions.

As the RISC-V ecosystem continues to grow, it is inspiring new innovations in custom processor design. Companies are increasingly moving away from proprietary architectures and adopting RISC-V to create processors tailored to specific AI, IoT, and HPC workloads. This shift towards open and customizable hardware solutions is paving the way for a future where energy-efficient computing can scale across diverse industries and applications.

The next step in the RISC-V revolution is scaling these technologies from prototypes to fully realized, mass-produced systems. As RISC-V continues to evolve, it will likely play an even larger role in shaping the future of energy-efficient computing, from AI accelerators to ultra-low-power edge devices.

The Future of Energy-Efficient Hardware

The future of low-power computing is not just about making hardware more energy-efficient; it's about designing processors that are smarter and more adaptable to the needs of the system. Innovations like RISC-V and other custom hardware solutions are making it possible to achieve higher performance with less energy consumption, marking the beginning of a new era in computing.

As energy efficiency becomes a primary concern for industries across the globe, the demand for specialized processors will continue to grow. From AI accelerators and neuromorphic chips to custom IoT solutions, the rise of domain-specific hardware will reshape how we think about computing. These innovations will drive the development of more sustainable, scalable, and efficient systems that can handle the increasingly complex demands of AI, IoT, and high-performance computing.

In the coming years, we can expect to see more advancements in hardware-software co-design, where both the hardware and software are optimized to work together seamlessly. This synergy will be essential for achieving the next generation of energy-efficient systems. By designing processors and algorithms that are tightly coupled, we can maximize performance while minimizing energy consumption.

As industries continue to adopt RISC-V and other low-power hardware solutions, the computing landscape will shift towards a future where efficiency is not just a design goal but a fundamental principle that underpins all technological innovation.

Chapter 5: Optimizing for Low Power – Software and Hardware Synergy

The Importance of Hardware-Software Integration

To achieve truly energy-efficient computing, it's not enough to simply focus on hardware or software alone. The real breakthroughs come when both are designed to work together, optimizing power usage across the system. A successful low-power computing system requires a balance between hardware capabilities and software efficiency. Without seamless integration, even the most advanced low-power hardware can be inefficient, and the best algorithms may not perform at their peak without the right hardware support.

Optimizing hardware for low power is only part of the equation. Software must also be tailored to the specific characteristics of the hardware it runs on. This synergy between hardware and software is essential for maximizing energy efficiency, as well as maintaining high performance. It's a dynamic approach, where both elements are optimized together to achieve the most power-efficient outcome.

Instruction Set Specialization

One key area where software and hardware synergy plays a vital role is in the instruction set of the processor. Traditional processors are designed to handle a wide range of tasks, which means they often consume unnecessary power when performing specialized operations. To address this, custom instruction sets tailored to specific workloads can significantly improve performance while reducing energy consumption.

For example, in AI and machine learning tasks, many computations involve repetitive operations like matrix multiplications and activation functions. Custom instructions designed specifically for these tasks can process them in fewer clock cycles, reducing the number of operations and, consequently, the energy required. RISC-V processors, with their modular nature, are particularly well-suited for creating these specialized instruction sets, allowing developers to design processors that efficiently handle specific AI tasks without the wastefulness of general-purpose computing.

In addition to specialized AI workloads, signal processing applications also benefit from customized instruction sets. By optimizing hardware to handle specific operations like Fast Fourier Transforms (FFTs) or digital filtering, these devices can perform real-time data processing with minimal energy expenditure, making them ideal for applications in IoT devices and embedded systems.

Memory Optimization

Another crucial component of energy efficiency is how memory is accessed and used. Memory operations are one of the largest consumers of energy in modern computing, especially when large volumes of data need to be constantly transferred between processors and memory. Memory optimization techniques are therefore key to improving energy efficiency without sacrificing performance.

One of the most effective approaches to memory optimization is near-memory computing, where computation is done as close to the memory as possible, reducing the need for frequent and power-intensive data transfers. By embedding computational units within memory systems, data can be processed locally, leading to faster results and lower energy consumption.

In addition to near-memory computing, optimizing memory hierarchy is also vital. In this approach, more frequently used data is stored in cache memory, reducing the need for long-distance memory fetches. This minimizes the power used in memory access while maintaining high data throughput, allowing systems to perform tasks like AI inference more efficiently.

The development of non-volatile memory (NVM) is another promising innovation in memory optimization. Unlike traditional dynamic random-access memory (DRAM), which requires constant power to retain data, NVM can store information without continuous energy input. This development has the potential to drastically reduce power consumption in low-power systems, making it ideal for devices that need to run on minimal energy for extended periods, like IoT devices and wearables.

Parallelism in Low Power Systems

Parallel processing is another crucial technique for achieving energy-efficient computing. Instead of relying on a single processor to handle all tasks, parallelism distributes the workload across multiple processing units, allowing tasks to be completed faster and more efficiently. This approach is especially important in AI and real-time applications, where the need for quick decision-making is paramount.

In low-power systems, parallelism is typically achieved by using multiple low-power cores that work together. These multi-core systems allow more work to be done at once, reducing the overall energy required compared to running everything on a single, high-power processor. Modern processors equipped with power-aware scheduling algorithms can activate the necessary cores depending on the workload, ensuring that idle cores are shut down to conserve energy.

Parallelism also enables more efficient use of specialized processors, such as AI accelerators, in low-power environments. These accelerators are optimized for specific tasks, such as neural network inference, and can be combined with general-purpose processors in a heterogeneous computing architecture. This allows for the intelligent distribution of tasks between different types of cores, ensuring that each task is handled by the most appropriate processing unit, thus improving both performance and energy efficiency.

Energy-Efficient Algorithms

While hardware optimizations are critical, the software running on these systems must also be optimized for energy efficiency. Energy-efficient algorithms are central to ensuring that AI models, machine learning frameworks, and general computing tasks consume the least amount of power possible while maintaining high performance.

One such optimization is model quantization, which involves reducing the precision of computations in AI models. By converting high-precision floating-point numbers into lower-bit integers, the system can process data with much lower energy consumption, all while maintaining an acceptable level of accuracy. This is particularly useful for edge AI applications, where resources are constrained.

Another technique for improving efficiency is neural network pruning, which removes redundant or unimportant connections in AI models. By simplifying the network, fewer computations are needed, reducing both the time it takes to process data and the energy required to do so.

In addition to these specific AI optimizations, adaptive scheduling algorithms can be used to adjust the computational intensity of tasks based on the power availability of the system. This means that when energy resources are low, the system can prioritize essential operations and delay or reduce less important tasks, extending the operational lifespan of the device.

A Future Built on Synergy

The future of low-power computing relies heavily on the synergy between hardware and software. As energy efficiency becomes a primary concern across all sectors, the need for optimized hardware and software working together will only grow. This will drive the development of smarter, more sustainable computing systems that can handle increasingly complex tasks without consuming excessive amounts of energy.

In this new era of computing, every part of the system will need to be designed with efficiency in mind. From custom processors and specialized instruction sets to energy-efficient algorithms and power-aware scheduling, every component will play a role in reducing the energy footprint of computing systems. The key to success will be building systems that are not just fast and powerful, but also intelligent in how they consume energy.

As we move forward, the goal will be to create a computing ecosystem where low-power designs are the default, not the exception. The combination of innovative hardware, software, and algorithmic advancements will pave the way for a future where technology can scale to meet the needs of a connected world without overwhelming energy resources.

Chapter 6: The Edge and Beyond

AI at the Edge: Small Devices, Big Impact

The growing demand for artificial intelligence (AI) is driving a shift from centralized computing in large data centers to decentralized, edge computing. This transition is particularly significant for AI applications that require real-time decision-making, such as autonomous systems, wearable devices, and smart infrastructure.

Edge devices process data locally, allowing for instant responses without relying on cloud-based systems. This shift not only reduces latency but also addresses power limitations, making real-time AI feasible in devices with limited energy resources.

One of the most exciting applications of edge AI is in wearables. Devices like smartwatches, fitness trackers, and medical monitors are increasingly capable of running sophisticated AI models to monitor health, track movement, and provide personalized recommendations—all while conserving battery life. These devices must be able to perform real-time computations efficiently and autonomously without constantly needing to offload data to the cloud.

Similarly, autonomous drones and robotic systems also benefit from edge AI. Drones used in agriculture, surveillance, or search-and-rescue missions rely on onboard AI to process video feeds, detect obstacles, and make flight decisions without waiting for cloud-based processing. Low-power AI processors enable these devices to operate for extended periods without draining their batteries, a crucial factor for their practical use in the real world.

The shift to edge AI is transforming industries by enabling smarter, faster, and more autonomous devices. These devices, although small and battery-powered, can perform complex tasks that once required massive computing power from the cloud. The future of AI at the edge will depend on developing more efficient hardware and algorithms that can run on these devices without compromising performance.

IoT and Smart Sensors

The Internet of Things (IoT) is another area where low-power AI is having a profound impact. IoT refers to the network of interconnected devices that collect and exchange data. These devices are often deployed in remote environments and need to operate autonomously for long periods, making energy efficiency essential. From smart agriculture sensors to environmental monitoring stations, IoT devices are becoming smarter, thanks to the integration of edge AI that allows them to process data locally.

In smart agriculture, sensors embedded in fields monitor soil moisture, temperature, and nutrient levels. These sensors use AI to analyze data and optimize irrigation schedules, ensuring that crops receive just the right amount of water. By processing data on the device itself, these sensors reduce the need for constant cloud communication, minimizing power consumption and increasing the overall efficiency of agricultural systems.

Similarly, wildlife tracking devices are benefiting from low-power AI. These sensors track animal movement patterns and environmental data without the need for frequent recharging. In these applications, long battery life is crucial for collecting data over extended periods. Low-power AI makes it possible to run these devices for weeks or even months on a single charge, revolutionizing how conservation efforts and wildlife research are conducted.

By processing data locally, IoT devices reduce the strain on network infrastructure and improve responsiveness. This also enables IoT systems to function in areas with limited or no connectivity, making them ideal for remote environments. The integration of AI into IoT is unlocking new possibilities in sectors like agriculture, healthcare, and environmental monitoring.

High-Performance Computing Systems

While edge AI and IoT devices face severe power constraints, high-performance computing (HPC) systems deal with a different challenge: managing the enormous power demands of large-scale AI workloads. Data centers and cloud computing infrastructures that support AI model training and deep learning simulations consume vast amounts of energy, which has become a growing concern. HPC systems require massive computational resources to handle the increasing complexity of AI models, but the need for energy-efficient solutions is more urgent than ever.

To address these challenges, AI-specific accelerators, such as tensor processing units (TPUs), RISC-V-based chips, and neuromorphic processors, are being integrated into HPC systems. These accelerators are designed to execute AI workloads more efficiently than traditional general-purpose CPUs and GPUs, significantly reducing power consumption while maintaining high computational performance.

Another promising strategy for improving the energy efficiency of HPC systems is the use of virtualization and dynamic power management. Virtualization allows multiple workloads to run on a shared infrastructure, making more efficient use of available resources. By consolidating workloads and dynamically adjusting power usage based on demand, these systems can optimize energy consumption while maintaining high throughput.

Additionally, advanced cooling techniques are being implemented in data centers to reduce the energy required for thermal management. Liquid cooling and immersion cooling are among the solutions being explored to keep systems running at peak performance without excessive energy waste. These innovations not only help reduce energy costs but also ensure that AI models can continue to evolve in a sustainable manner.

Scaling the Low-Power Revolution

The transition to low-power computing is not just limited to edge devices and IoT sensors—it's impacting all layers of the AI ecosystem. From high-performance computing systems to wearable devices, energy-efficient technologies are making AI more accessible, scalable, and sustainable.

In the future, AI systems will need to function seamlessly across diverse environments, from cloud data centers to remote IoT devices. The key to scaling low-power AI is hardware-software co-design—optimizing both the underlying hardware and the software running on it to work together efficiently. By focusing on power-efficient AI models, specialized processors, and intelligent resource allocation, we can ensure that AI continues to grow without overwhelming energy resources.

This revolution in low-power computing will enable AI to thrive in new applications that were once thought to be out of reach. Whether it's in healthcare, agriculture, or autonomous systems, low-power AI will drive innovation in ways that were not possible with traditional computing models.

The age of smarter, more energy-efficient technology is here, and its impact will continue to unfold across industries and everyday life.

Chapter 7: Overcoming the Trade-offs –

Achieving Performance and Efficiency: The Cost of Low Power

In the world of computing, achieving a balance between performance and energy efficiency has always been a significant challenge. For decades, the mindset in computing has been simple: more power equals more performance. The more powerful your processor, the faster your system can execute tasks. However, this traditional approach has led to an unsustainable reliance on high-energy-consuming systems.

In the past, power-efficient computing was often associated with lower performance. Devices designed to consume less energy, such as embedded microcontrollers and low-power processors, were often too slow to handle complex tasks like AI inference, real-time analytics, and high-performance computing (HPC). The belief that saving energy meant sacrificing performance was deeply ingrained in the industry. But this perception is quickly changing.

Today's energy-efficient architectures are proving that high performance and low power can coexist. By developing smarter, more adaptable systems, engineers are finding ways to optimize performance while reducing energy consumption. The key is to move away from brute-force computing and toward a more intelligent approach that maximizes efficiency without compromising speed.

Innovations in Computational Efficiency

One of the most exciting breakthroughs in energy-efficient computing is the development of task-specific accelerators—processors designed to handle specific workloads. Traditional processors are general-purpose, meaning they consume excess power when performing specialized tasks. Task-specific accelerators, such as AI accelerators, digital signal processors (DSPs), and neuromorphic chips, are optimized to perform particular tasks with minimal energy consumption.

For instance, AI accelerators are designed to perform neural network computations much more efficiently than general-purpose CPUs or GPUs. These accelerators can handle the massive parallelism required for deep learning without consuming the same amount of energy as traditional processors. The result is a system that can run advanced AI models faster and with significantly less power.

In addition to task-specific hardware, neural network quantization and model pruning are key innovations for improving computational efficiency. These techniques reduce the complexity of AI models without sacrificing accuracy, allowing them to run on low-power processors. Quantization reduces the precision of computations, lowering power usage while still maintaining acceptable levels of performance. Pruning removes unnecessary connections from neural networks, decreasing the computational load and further reducing power consumption.

Another breakthrough is event-driven processing, a method that activates computing resources only when a specific task requires attention. Traditional processors consume power continuously, even when idle. In contrast, event-driven systems only use power when triggered by an event, such as a change in data or the need for processing. This is particularly beneficial in low-power environments, such as edge devices and IoT systems, where the ability to operate autonomously for extended periods is essential.

System-Level Optimizations

Achieving energy efficiency in computing systems is not just about individual components; it also requires optimization at the system level. From power management to workload scheduling, every part of the system must work together to minimize energy consumption without sacrificing performance.

One of the most important aspects of system-level energy optimization is dynamic power management. In systems where multiple processors are used, managing the activation and deactivation of cores based on workload intensity can dramatically reduce power consumption. This technique, often used in multi-core processors, ensures that only the necessary cores are active at any given time, preventing unnecessary energy waste.

Another system-level optimization is thermal management. High-performance processors generate significant heat, which requires energy-intensive cooling solutions. Innovations such as liquid cooling and immersion cooling help mitigate this issue by improving heat dissipation, allowing processors to run at peak performance without excessive power consumption for cooling.

In cloud computing and data center environments, virtualization plays a critical role in optimizing power distribution. Virtualization enables multiple workloads to run on a shared infrastructure, allowing resources to be used more efficiently and minimizing idle power consumption. Dynamic scheduling and resource allocation ensure that systems only consume the energy needed to handle the current workload, further reducing overall power use.

Balancing Power and Performance for the Future

The future of computing will not be defined by raw performance alone, but by the ability to balance power and efficiency. As AI, IoT, and high-performance computing continue to evolve, the demand for systems that can scale without overwhelming energy resources will increase. The ability to design systems that intelligently allocate power based on workload and energy availability will be key to achieving this balance.

To successfully achieve this balance, the hardware-software synergy will be crucial. Optimized software running on specialized hardware will ensure that computing resources are used efficiently while still delivering high performance. Developers will need to focus on creating software that is power-aware, capable of dynamically adjusting to the available resources while maintaining optimal performance.

In addition, the integration of AI-driven power management and adaptive computing models will help guide the next generation of computing. These systems will be capable of learning from past usage patterns and adjusting their power consumption strategies accordingly. By predicting power needs in real-time and allocating resources efficiently, AI can help drive energy-efficient computing to new heights.

The Road Ahead

While there are still challenges to overcome, the path toward energy-efficient computing is becoming clearer. Innovations in hardware, software, and system-level optimizations are transforming the way we think about computing. As the demand for energy-efficient AI continues to grow, the future of computing will depend on systems that not only perform faster but also consume less power.

In the coming years, we can expect to see more widespread adoption of low-power systems in sectors such as healthcare, automotive, and industrial automation. From AI-driven medical diagnostics to self-driving cars, the low-power revolution will enable smarter, more sustainable technologies that can handle increasingly complex tasks without overwhelming our planet's energy resources.

The shift from power-hungry computing to intelligent, energy-efficient systems is already underway, and those who can successfully navigate this transition will lead the charge in shaping the future of technology.

Chapter 8: The Future of Low Power in AI and Computing

Trends and Predictions

The landscape of computing is rapidly evolving, driven by the growing need for AI, minimal latency, and energy efficiency. As AI systems become more complex and ubiquitous, low-power computing will continue to take center stage. In the next decade, we will likely see energy-efficient AI becoming the default across all industries, influencing the design of processors, accelerators, and distributed computing architectures.

One significant trend is the continued decentralization of AI workloads. Cloud-based AI has dominated for years, but this model is being increasingly replaced by hybrid solutions that blend cloud, edge, and on-device computing. By processing data closer to where it is generated, these hybrid systems offer faster AI inference, reduced data transmission costs, and improved privacy and security. As a result, edge AI will grow exponentially, empowering devices to function without relying on constant cloud connectivity.

Another key trend is the convergence of AI with energy-efficient chip designs. Companies are prioritizing the development of custom AI hardware, such as neuromorphic processors, tensor-based accelerators, and low-power RISC-V cores, to maximize performance per watt. As domain-specific architectures (DSAs) become more common, they will enable AI to be more efficient, ensuring that real-time processing remains scalable and sustainable across a wide range of applications.

Self-learning AI models will also play a critical role in the future. These AI systems will be able to adjust their complexity based on real-time power availability and workload demand, making them ideal for applications where energy is limited, such as in autonomous robotics, smart agriculture, and remote sensing. With these advancements, low-power AI will thrive in areas once thought to be impractical for AI technologies.

Emerging Technologies

The future of low-power computing goes beyond current trends and innovations. Revolutionary breakthroughs are on the horizon that will push the boundaries of energy-efficient AI and intelligent automation. Some of these emerging technologies include quantum computing, neuromorphic computing, and biological computing, which could all dramatically transform the field of energy-efficient computation.

Quantum computing represents one of the most exciting frontiers in energy-efficient computing. Quantum computers process information using quantum bits (qubits), allowing them to perform multiple calculations at once. While still in its early stages, quantum AI has the potential to solve complex problems—like optimization tasks and cryptographic analysis—with far lower energy consumption than traditional computers. The introduction of quantum AI will redefine how energy-intensive computations are carried out, enabling exponentially faster calculations with significantly reduced energy use.

Neuromorphic computing, which mimics the way the human brain processes information, is another groundbreaking technology. By using biological synapses and neurons, neuromorphic chips can execute AI tasks more efficiently than traditional von Neumann architectures. This approach could enable AI to operate with drastically lower energy consumption, making it ideal for edge applications in autonomous systems and real-time machine perception. Companies like Intel, IBM, and BrainChip are already developing neuromorphic processors that could revolutionize the way AI interacts with the world around it.

Additionally, biological computing and molecular electronics offer radical alternatives to silicon-based systems. Using DNA-based computing and protein nanostructures, researchers are exploring ways to store and process information using far less energy. These biological systems could lead to computers that operate at near-biological energy levels, offering a promising future where computing systems require minimal energy inputs to run sophisticated models.

Global Impacts

The shift to low-power AI is not just a technological advancement; it is a global imperative that will have far-reaching implications for society, the environment, and the economy. As energy consumption in computing continues to rise, it is essential to develop systems that can scale without overwhelming the planet's resources.

AI-driven energy efficiency is already playing a pivotal role in efforts to combat climate change. Technologies like smart grids, predictive climate modeling, and AI-powered resource management systems are helping governments and industries optimize energy consumption, reduce waste, and transition to renewable energy sources. By making AI models more energy-efficient, these technologies can contribute to global sustainability goals while maintaining high levels of computational power.

Low-power AI is also making a profound impact in healthcare. Wearable biosensors, powered by ultra-efficient AI, can continuously track health metrics such as heart rate, blood oxygen levels, and movement patterns.

These devices enable more proactive healthcare interventions, improving patient outcomes while conserving energy. As AI advances, it will continue to revolutionize healthcare by making diagnostic tools, wearable devices, and real-time monitoring systems more efficient and accessible.

Autonomous systems are another sector benefiting from low-power AI. In electric vehicles and robotic agriculture, the ability to perform complex tasks using minimal energy is transforming industries.

AI-powered agricultural systems can help optimize crop production while reducing environmental impact, while self-driving cars can extend battery range and improve overall efficiency. By minimizing energy consumption, low-power AI is enabling the development of more sustainable, scalable technologies that can operate independently for extended periods.

On a global scale, the rise of low-power AI is promoting digital equity and making technology more accessible. AI systems that were once confined to high-end devices are now being integrated into low-cost, energy-efficient solutions that can be deployed in regions with limited energy infrastructure. This democratization of technology ensures that communities in developing areas can benefit from innovations like intelligent automation, healthcare advancements, and real-time connectivity.

The economic impact of energy-efficient computing is also significant. By reducing energy consumption in data centers, IoT networks, and AI-driven industries, businesses can achieve substantial cost savings while lowering their carbon footprints. Governments are increasingly investing in energy-efficient AI research, recognizing that sustainable growth and technological progress go hand in hand.

A Future Powered by Intelligence, Not Excess

As we look toward the future, the most important shift in computing will not be toward more powerful machines, but toward more intelligent and efficient systems. The days of power-hungry supercomputers are coming to an end. Instead, the next generation of AI and computing systems will be designed to do more with less.

The innovations highlighted in this book—from low-power AI accelerators and RISC-V processors to parallel architectures and AI-driven power management—are just the beginning. The future of AI will be defined by systems that are not only faster and smarter but also more energy-efficient. As energy-efficient computing becomes the new norm, technology will scale to meet the demands of a connected world without overwhelming our planet's resources.

The low-power revolution is here, and its impact will be felt across every sector, from healthcare and transportation to agriculture and energy. The challenge ahead is clear: to make computing smarter, we must make it more efficient. The future of AI will not be defined by how much power we consume, but by how intelligently we use it.

Conclusion

We've spent decades building machines that are faster, bigger, and more powerful. But here's the catch—raw power comes at a cost. Our data centers gulp electricity. Our devices demand more juice. And every new AI breakthrough risks pushing us further into an unsustainable tech future.

Now, things are changing. Quietly. Radically. We're entering a new era where the real flex isn't brute-force computing—it's efficiency. The smartest tech of tomorrow isn't the one that burns the most watts—it's the one that does the job with barely a sizzle.

This isn't some greenwashed dream. It's already happening. Tiny processors are pulling off tasks once reserved for supercomputers. AI is moving from the cloud to your wrist, your fridge, your front door. And it's not just surviving out there—it's thriving, thanks to clever design and serious innovation.

We've seen RISC-V chips kick open the door to custom, open-source hardware. We've watched AI accelerators strip away the fluff and focus on the essentials. And software? It's slimming down too. Leaner algorithms, energy-aware code, and smarter scheduling are making our devices not just faster, but wiser.

And here's the real kicker: low-power tech isn't just about performance or cost savings—it's about access. With systems that run longer, cooler, and lighter, we can bring powerful computing to places where infrastructure is scarce and energy is precious. We're talking smarter farms, cleaner hospitals, safer cities—all powered by tech that knows how to pace itself.

The low-power revolution isn't about sacrificing performance. It's about redefining it. It's about saying goodbye to the old model of "more is better" and saying hello to a future where better is smarter.

So what now?

For engineers: the mission is to build with intention, not excess.

For coders: write code that runs hard but sips soft.

For decision-makers: invest in innovation that doesn't leave a carbon footprint the size of a crater.

Because this isn't just a trend—it's the blueprint for what's next.

We don't need louder machines. We need clever ones.

Ones that last longer. Think faster. Work smarter.

The power game has changed.

And this time, less really is more.

Appendix

You've reached the end of the journey—now here's your quick-reference guide. This appendix breaks down the core technologies, terms, and concepts that have been driving the low-power revolution. Use it as your backstage pass to the smarter, leaner future of computing.

RISC-V

An open-source instruction set architecture that's simple, modular, and highly customizable. Unlike traditional, locked-down processor architectures, RISC-V gives designers the freedom to build exactly what they need—ideal for efficient, low-power designs.

DVFS (Dynamic Voltage and Frequency Scaling)

A power-saving strategy that adjusts a processor's voltage and clock speed on the fly based on workload demands. It's a smarter way to stretch battery life and reduce energy use during idle periods.

Power Gating

Rather than keeping all processor parts running all the time, power gating shuts off unused components. It's one of the most effective ways to reduce static power consumption, especially in systems with multiple cores.

Model Quantization

A method of simplifying AI models by using lower-precision numbers. Quantization helps reduce the size and energy use of neural networks, making them better suited for edge and mobile devices.

Neural Network Pruning

This technique removes unnecessary weights and connections in a neural network, trimming it down without sacrificing much accuracy. The result? Faster processing and lower power demands.

Near-Memory Computing

Traditional systems waste power by constantly moving data between memory and processors. Near-memory computing processes data closer to where it's stored, reducing energy use and boosting speed.

Neuromorphic Computing

Inspired by the human brain, neuromorphic chips use neuron-like structures to process information. They're incredibly efficient at handling sensory tasks and pattern recognition with minimal power.

Edge AI

Artificial intelligence that runs on local devices instead of the cloud. From smart cameras to wearables, edge AI enables real-time decisions with minimal latency and maximum power efficiency.

IoT (Internet of Things)

A massive network of connected sensors, devices, and everyday objects. As IoT grows, efficient computing is crucial to keep these devices running reliably, especially in remote or power-limited environments.

Task-Specific Accelerators

Processors built for specific jobs, like AI inference or video processing. By focusing on a single task, they operate far more efficiently than general-purpose CPUs.

Thermal Management

Keeping systems cool is critical for performance and efficiency. Techniques like liquid cooling and intelligent workload distribution help maintain optimal temperatures and prevent energy waste.